Innovation on
Two wheels

Conversations with
Arun Firodia

Innovation on Two Wheels

Conversations with Arun Firodia

First Edition - 2014

© Arun Firodia & Publisher, 2014

ISBN 978-93-83572-12-0

Published by:

Vishwakarma Publications
"Shreemangal" Building, 5th Floor,
251, Budhwar Peth, Near City Post,
Opp. Bank of India, Pune - 411002.
Phone: +91-20-24498111
Email: info@vpindia.co.in
Website: www.vpindia.co.in

Cover Design, Typeset and Layout:
Media Sphere Communications Pvt. Ltd.
www.mediasphere.co.in

Printed by:
Repro India Limited,
Mumbai.

" *The best ideas lose their owners and take on lives of their own.* "

Table of Contents

Foreword

Arun Firodia is a rare combination of a hands-on engineer, a game changing innovator and a bold visionary thinker. His book 'Innovations on Two Wheels' reflects all these great qualities of my most revered friend, Arun, in an incredibly lucid way.

What I found particularly fascinating is that the book shows vividly that the ideas that are being looked at as new breakthroughs in our thinking, are something that Arun conceived and practiced over three decades ago!

During the last five years the dictionary of innovation is changing. There are new terms such as frugal innovation, inclusive innovation, reverse innovation, Gandhian innovation and so on. They all signify getting more from less for more people – not just more profit. But if one reads Arun's book carefully, one will find that all that is being preached today is something that was demonstrated by Arun and his team around four decades ago!

The Tata Nano car created so much of excitement, since for the first time the common man could make a transition from a two wheeler to a four wheeler, which was safe, fuel efficient, but also affordable. If one looks at the inspirational story of Luna described in the book, then one finds the equally challenging shift for a common man from bicycle to an affordable scooter using the same objective and strategy.

Creation of Tata Nano car inspired a book titled 'Nanovation' by Kevin & Jaenie Freiberg and Dain Duston, three US citizens. I wish there was a book titled 'Lunavation' three decades ago, since the basic principle of 'affordable excellence' was embedded so deeply into the making of Luna.

Luna is such a fascinating case study. It shows how combination of scarcity and constraint on one hand and aspiration and ambition on the other, can lead to innovations, which can benefit millions. More importantly, it shows how 'total innovation', that involves the complete journey from mind to market place is important. Luna was a technological innovation but backed up by a superb marketing innovation. In fact I have always said that beyond the technological innovation, other innovations such as business model, business process, organizational, workflow and policy innovation are equally important.

I believe the story of making Luna should become the textbook lesson for engineering schools across the country to illustrate as to how innovative thinking, which combines the concepts of affordability, sustainability and quality, can be big winners in the market place today. The case of Kinetic Honda, in a different context, has also some fascinating lessons.

Arun is a technopreneur. His advice in the book on building a company comes from his own experience. Today, we need to create young entrepreneurs, who will not be asking for jobs – but creating jobs. Arun's messages in the book will go a long way in building new mindsets of entrepreneurs.

I do hope that the book, which represents the pioneering contributions of one of the greatest engineering innovators and technopreneurs of our time, will reach the nooks and corners of the country and will inspire thousands of young innovators and entrepreneurs.

R.A. Mashelkar

Preface

India in the early 1970s was a country in transition. Entrepreneurship was a tough proposition, considering that we had gained independence barely 25 years ago. Innovation was alien to any business enterprise. Thankfully though, we had visionaries who picked up the gauntlet to take unprecedented risks to create business and market segments, which did not exist before. They pioneered products that bore the stamp of a lifestyle of Modern India.

One such dynamic entrepreneur and innovator is Mr Arun Firodia. He spearheaded a social revolution in India by changing the way India moves on roads, for the personal convenience of commuters, who were otherwise at the whims and fancies of an inefficient public transport system. The stories of Luna, Kinetic Honda and various other products that he dreamt and brought to life are testimony to his commitment to excellence, innovation and citizen convenience.

This book aims to capture his drive for innovation, his desire for excellence and his vision in putting India on the global map of innovation.

At a sprightly 70 years of age, Mr Firodia continues to be a regular at work, travelling to his Ahmednagar factory, from Pune, twice in a week or more. He is also involved in a wide range of activities outside his responsibilities at Kinetic Group.

The Energy in Kinetic

Innovation isn't inborn. It needs to be cultivated. After coming out with flying colours from IIT Powai, Arun Firodia spent time in the US before returning home. It was the early 1970s when his father, H K Firodia, decided to sow the seed for a unique two-wheeler personalised transport, which would be affordable to the common man. Armed with knowledge, passion and the fiery and visionary desire of his father who wanted his only son to come back to India to head this project, a young Arun set about trying to understand what it is that the Indian consumer wanted.

That was an era when necessity took precedence over luxury. Not surprisingly, products to come out of the

Kinetic Engineering stables were to be practical and affordable to the common man! Iconic brands such as the Luna and the Kinetic Honda were born out of the visionary and entrepreneurial skills of the Firodias. It is these two vehicles that changed the way India commuted. If the Luna was a smooth and convenient graduation from the bicycle, the Kinetic Honda kick-started lifestyle-commuting, patronised therefore by the fair gender in large numbers. The sleek scooter also depicted an image of a reliable 'family' vehicle. Both the two-wheelers came to be seen as global quality products for the aspiring Indian, for their economical and driving convenience.

Arun Firodia's indelible stamp of quality and hard work manifests in various aspects of engineering, product planning and marketing.

Not one to sit on his laurels, Mr Arun Firodia continues to lead the way in product innovation. Be it the involvement in creating a 90-seater aircraft or a cooking machine or working on fuel sticks that are 100% eco-friendly, his thirst for innovation is insatiable!

While two-wheelers may be what he's best known for, he has also led the development of many other products including the all-in-one computer and TV, the Merlin.

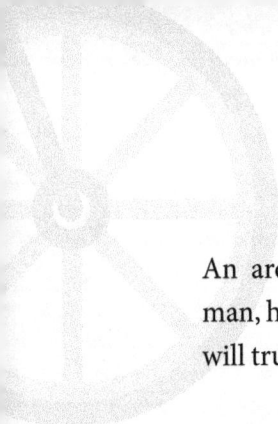

An ardent supporter of innovation for the common man, he continues to tirelessly work for innovations that will truly make a difference in the daily lives of millions.

In the next few chapters Mr Firodia takes the reader through his career studded with innovations – in products, in marketing and in organization development.

What is Innovation?

R& D in a laboratory and innovation in the marketplace are two different things. A product developed in the laboratory will become an innovation i.e. succeed in the marketplace if R&D and marketing work together in harmony.

A large amount of R&D is often confined to the four walls of the laboratory and rarely enters the practical arena of the marketplace. Winning a patent is the end of the lifecycle for many an innovation. This, however, is not truly innovation. To convert research into a marketing success you need to take it to the market as a product. Innovation not only requires R&D whether it is your own or someone else's, but it is pertinent to have the ability to convert it into a usable product for the masses.

An innovation has its genesis in the marketplace. Is there a need for your product? How wide will the appeal and uptake of your product be? How sustainable is it? Can it evolve into something bigger and better as time goes by? These are considerations that need to be taken into account for any product.

Listen to the Market

The Luna moped was born out of a conversation between Dr. Vikram Sarabhai who was the then chairman of the Indian Space Research Organisation (ISRO) and my father, Mr H.K Firodia when they were once, travelling together in a plane. My father introduced himself and told Dr Sarabhai that his Company made "scooters."

Being a visionary scientist, Dr Sarabhai made a suggestion that was to set the course for our Company in the years to come. He told my father to make scooters "for the common man" that would cost half of what they did at the time. That set my father thinking about such a venture.

This wasn't the first time my father had contemplated making a vehicle for the common man. Years ago, when he was in the USA for his studies, he had seen an advertisement in the newspapers about a company that manufactured foldable scooters. The idea was simple. When a paratrooper landed, he could make away easily with this foldable vehicle. The vehicle would be lightweight but could ride over rough terrain. So my father thought such a vehicle would be an ideal one for the common man in India. Unfortunately, when he finally tracked down the manufacturer, he found out that the company had ceased operations. The end of the World War II had brought about its end. However, the thought of a lightweight scooter had registered in his mind. The meeting with Dr Sarabhai re-ignited his desire to create a vehicle for the common man.

Innovation has to be thought of in conjunction with the marketplace. The market is not going to come up to you and tell you what it wants! But its needs are important. The only way you can achieve this is by being in touch with the market. You need to listen to what the market is telling you, filter it and apply it.

The market will never tell you exactly what it wants. There will only be clues! Like a good detective, you need to put two-and-two together and give the market what it wants. The reason it can't tell you exactly what it wants is because the market doesn't always know itself. This is where the visionary and the innovator come to the fore, as they need to catch the pulse of the buyer. Understanding, interpreting and implementing the needs of the market is what makes a successful product.

Timing should be Right

In the early 1970s, India was making a transition from a poor country to a developing one. Basic infrastructure was available in the country. After years of dominance by public sector, the private enterprise was making its presence felt and being encouraged. The Middle Class came into prominence. Cities were growing. People could no longer commute to their work place on bicycles. There arose a need for a low cost vehicle that would provide mobility to the common man. The timing was just right for the Luna to be introduced. It almost seemed like the right time to me – looking back, I now feel, that, if it was introduced 10-15 years earlier it would have been ahead of the times and if it had been introduced 10-15 years later, it would have been too late.

Great concepts are of no practical use in the marketplace if they are introduced before their time. Battery-operated vehicles originated 100 years ago even before people used such vehicles. However, they did not see the marketplace because they did not have the required range for travel.

Besides, the battery was too bulky and expensive. Petrol became cheap and electricity was expensive for a very long time in the 20th century. A natural result of this was that vehicles ran on petrol and not electricity. However, today, this has reversed and there is a natural inclination towards developing electric-powered vehicles over fossil fuels that are depleting. Batteries have become smaller and less expensive and it won't be long before lithium-iron batteries have the ability to store energy that is enough to power a vehicle! So nearly 100 years after the idea was first thought of, battery-operated vehicles may become a mass product today!

The Luna

A t that time in 1970, I was working in the USA on development of Microprocessor. My father wrote to me asking me to come back to India, because he wanted to manufacture a moped! I asked him what a moped was. "A vehicle for the common man" was his cryptic answer. Visualising that it would be something like a Volkswagen Beetle I agreed. I sought permission to return to India after six months, as I needed to wind up my affairs in the USA. It was only when I landed home in India that I found out what a moped really meant. It stood for "mo"torised and "ped"alled vehicle. So, it was somewhere, between a bicycle and a scooter. He had already set up the project. A team was also recruited under Mr Daljit Singh Bomrah. My cousin Mr Abhay

Firodia took a keen interest in the project. I was an electronics engineer, not a mechanical one! But as always, my father assured me his support and we set about making the Luna.

What were the target specifications of Luna?

It needed to be:
○ Cheap enough to own (ideally to be priced at half the price of a scooter i.e. below Rs 2000)
○ Lightweight (below 50 kg)
○ Easy to maintain and run (fuel economy of 60 km to a litre)
○ To be completely indigenous – not possess any imported components or raw material.

The project was to be made:
○ Without foreign collaboration
○ Without imported machinery
○ Was to be set up in our home town Ahmednagar, an industrially backward area. (The last stipulation was at the instance of my uncle Mr. N.K.Firodia, the well known freedom fighter)

Thus, a new Company "Kinetic Engineering Ltd" was set up to manufacture Luna, with an initial share capital of Rs 15 Lakh!

Fulfil Consumer Needs

We went around meeting mechanics and users asking them what they wanted to see in such a vehicle. A common answer was "something that is easy to repair and maintain."

A major problem that mechanics and users faced was the need to take down the engine for every repair. This was costly for the user and time-consuming for the mechanic. Could we avoid taking down the engine if the clutch or gear box required attention? Yes, we could. We separated the engine, gear box and clutch to solve this problem.

Petrol in those days was heavily adulterated. As a result, the cylinder head and exhaust port of the engine used to develop a lot of carbon deposit. So every two to three months, they needed cleaning. Mechanics told us that the carbon deposit problem was a major irritant to most users and should be addressed in our vehicle. So we made the engine horizontal and pointed its exhaust port downwards. As a result, cleaning could be done in a matter of minutes.

Another issue was the poor quality of roads. This used to result in punctured tyres regularly! To fix this, the entire wheel had to be removed. We designed the mounting of the rear wheel so that a punctured tube could be taken out for repair without dismantling the wheel.

As we could address these and other issues, we made Luna a vehicle that appealed to consumers and mechanics alike.

Product Innovation

The Luna is responsible for many innovations and firsts in the Indian auto sector. For this, we took inspiration from diverse unconnected areas.

We had set ourselves many goals when we started to design Luna. Our first goal was to keep the cost of Luna to half of what a scooter cost back then. A Scooter weighed 100 Kg. So we thought that the weight of Luna must not exceed 50 Kg. That way, maybe the cost target would be met, we thought. Borrowing from the principles of monocoque aircraft frames, we made a box chassis for the Luna where the strength comes from the box design and not from the thickness of the metal sheets. We then decided to create the petrol tank within this box itself. That obviously saved weight. Further, the engine requires constant supply of cool, clean air, but atmospheric air in India has a lot of dust which can damage the engine. We sensed that if the air can be taken from a higher point, it would be cleaner. So we took it from underneath the seat through the box frame and gave it to the carburettor. Maximizing the utility of the box being our aim, we placed the tool kit also inside it!

To further reduce weight, we decided to use plastic in our vehicle. Back then, Indians were not fond of plastic because of the notion that it didn't last. But we decided to go ahead anyways. This was the first time in India that plastic was used in vehicles.

When using plastic, you need just one injection mould and that's it! The plastic granules can be moulded into the required shape and so no additional fastening or welding is required. Apart from these benefits, from the manufacturing point of view, the users get the benefit of a lighter vehicle that would automatically be more fuel efficient. Also, in case of damage to the vehicle, the user won't have to spend time and money in denting and painting but could just replace the covers and that would be cheaper than sending the vehicle to the garage. Once we realised that plastic can be used for making the headlamp, the idea of using it for housing the speed-ometer as well, caught our fancy. This would mean that we had a two-in-one or even a three-in-one utility on the headlamp that would save space and material cost. While this was happening, our 'greed' for getting more from plastic and more from the headlamp was growing! Next to be ensconsed within the headlamp was the horn!

And soon enough, the power switch for the headlamp also found a home here! While it seemed like greediness initially, these decisions have side benefits. For example, housing the headlamp switch right there also helped us to save on length of wiring.

There were many other product innovations. Concealed engine with forced air cooling; sheet metal brake drum with single rear brake shoe; front fork in steel tubes; dry clutch; belt transmission; disengagement lever to pedal the Luna if required; lifting hook to carry Luna up the stairs; front wheel of 28 spokes; sintered cam; die cast thin flywheel magneto; encapsulated and protected H.T. coil........ all of these were possible because we were free to innovate. We were not tied down by any Licensing conditions of "no change without permission of Licensor" as we had no foreign collaborator. This was indeed a blessing in disguise.

Technology from Business Associates

In terms of weight, cost and aesthetics; the decision to use plastic, yielded benefits. The technology of Engineering Plastics was not yet developed in India. Plastic was mostly used for household items like buckets. This posed a challenge for us. Here our business associates took up the challenge.

There is a company called Bright Brothers. At the time, they were focused on manufacturing household items but were also keen to get into *engineering plastics*. We met with their chief engineer – Mr. Khan. When we explained to him that we want to create plastic head-lamps, he was surprised. It wasn't something that was done before. However, he was keen to diversify from buckets and combs into engineering plastics! His initiative helped us create acrylic lens and ABS reflectors, for the first time in India.

We also needed dies to make the box chassis, but we had no tool room to make the dies. My father took us to meet Mr. Sumant Moolgaonkar of TELCO. We asked for his help to make the dies and told him that we could only pay the material cost! Much to our gratitude, he agreed! We had crossed the next hurdle!

With the moulds and dies in place, we still needed to set-up the factory. To mass manufacture, you need special purpose machines. One machine was required for the crankcase of the engine and another for the gear box. Yet another machine was needed to machine the block and another for the head. Instead of multiple machines, we decided to explore if just one machine could do all this for us since we could afford only one machine in our budget!

Seemingly impossible, we were happy when our chief engineer Mr Bomrah told us that making such a machine is indeed possible. Once again we went to my father for help. He introduced us to Dr S.M. Patil from Hindustan Machine Tools (HMT) and asked whether such a machine could indeed be made. Dr Patil sent his people over, for a detailed understanding and soon enough, work on the machine began. And lo and behold, we got one multipurpose SPM! We had succeeded in reducing the cost of machinery in one fell swoop! This was an innovation that the public would perhaps never know about.

SKF Pimpri had a German M.D. He took special interest in the design of the engine and helped us to select appropriate bearings and decide the tolerances of the bore to house them. Dr Don Morris, founder of Morris Electronics helped us design the coils and magneto to meet the lighting requirements of various countries.

Our next challenge was the painting of the vehicles. Creating a paint shop is an expensive affair. It needs a booth, a boiler and a heated oven. Once again, our meagre budget stood in the way. Like they say, where there is a will, there will be an innovation!

We decided to opt for infra-red heating. This offered us a simple advantage. You don't need to heat the whole oven. The oven is used only to accommodate the components. The infrared bulb directly heats paint on the component, like in a microwave oven. For this solution, though, we needed gas, which meant expensive installation! Once again, we found a rather ingenuous solution!

We built the oven ourselves to save cost. During this process, we realised that infrared bulbs actually heated up the components faster thereby making it more economically viable! Unfortunately, this technique is still not widely used despite its benefits.

Too much of a good thing!

In our enthusiasm of producing an Indian vehicle, we overlooked some regulatory issues. In the 1970s, every Company was given a "Capacity" which you could not exceed. We did! A case was filed against us by the Monopoly and Restricted Trade Practices Commission for producing more than our allotted capacity! That, we were using only locally made components and raw materials and not importing any machinery nor transferring any "royalty" abroad, was not considered! As per rules, this penalty applied to companies which had foreign collaborations and brought in foreign exchange.

Ongoing Innovations

Because Luna had to operate on Indian roads, we had to keep improving it as the feedback came. We also went through our internal feedback. Our test rider was asked to travel a distance of 300 km per day. The idea was to cover a distance of one Lakh kms in a year. We realized that the distance from Ahmednagar to Pune and back is exactly 300 km. We asked our test rider to start from Ahmednagar in the morning with a milk can every day, deliver it to us in Pune and return. Since this test drive was by a real person with income attached to end of the task, we were sure of real-world inputs and feedback. It also helped us that he brought us fresh milk every morning from there!

Testing in controlled facilities will give you some inputs, but when you test in an uncontrolled, real-world scenario, the feedback you get and implement makes a big difference. On the basis of feedback, we made the required changes which ensured that the Luna stayed a great vehicle, in terms of sturdiness and convenience to the owner. The biggest testimony to the success of Luna was during my visit to the Piaggio factory in Italy. They had showcased a Luna there! When I inquired as to what prompted them to do so, I was told that a vehicle which withstood Indian conditions needs to be studied! Coming from the inventors of the scooter, this was a huge compliment to our efforts!

The Kinetic Honda

L una gave mobility to the 'common man' in the seventies and eighties. However, there arose a new opportunity in the nineties to cater to women who had begun venturing out of their homes. Their mobility included stirring out not only for jobs but in multi tasks like dropping children to school, shopping and so on. They yearned for a vehicle of their own. Much to their delight, we offered them the Kinetic Honda. A vehicle, which had no gears, did not need a kick-start and which was light in weight. It was perceived as an ideal companion for women.

Since the late 18th century, Pune has always been known for social reforms for women. Whether it was women's education or re-marriage after widowhood, women's emancipation movements flourished in this city. Women of Pune rode cycles and vied for jobs with men. Maybe that is why we were subconsciously looking for such a product. We found it in the Honda's stable. We entered into a Joint Venture (JV) with Honda to bring this easy-to-drive scooter in the market. It brought about a veritable social revolution in the lives of women.

Marketing Innovations

A new product line is either disruptive in its nature or adds great value to an existing way of life. The Luna, perhaps, was one of the few products that created a new way of life and disrupted existing norms.

Positioning

Although Luna was conceived as a "common man's scooter," we had not positioned it as such. The Luna owner was an upwardly mobile person, although he belonged to the middle class fraternity. He would not like to be branded as a "common man" just because he owned a Luna. So, we positioned Luna as a vehicle which was a time-saver and more importantly a fuel saver.

Incidentally, when the Luna was launched, a Middle East Oil crisis had steeply raised the price of Petrol. In those days, TV wasn't as prevalent. Since Radio was the medium with the widest reach, we created a straightforward radio jingle for Luna:

> *Samay bachaiye, petrol bachaiye.*
> *Ek litre mein 60 km jaanewali Luna*

However, we also did not want Luna to be seen as a miser's vehicle. In order to enhance the status of the Luna buyer, we made special efforts to sell it to high profile opinion leaders like Doctors, Professors and Air Hostesses. Dr Jayashree, my wife, who is a paediatrician, could cut ice with the lady doctors' segment.

We used a similar approach when we launched the Kinetic Honda. We never positioned it as a 'Ladies' vehicle nor as a 'technologically advanced scooter.' Our tagline read: "**simpler, safer, superior.**" If we had positioned it as a Ladies' scooter we would have lost the 'family market'. Mind you, in those days each family could afford only one scooter. Nor did we want to overawe the buyer with technical jargon and features. We just told him we had something better to make his life easier.

"No Foreign Collaboration" Challenge

While the petrol crisis was a boon for us when we launched the Luna, other challenges did abound! Firstly, we did not have a foreign collaboration! Luna was the first and, for many years thereafter, the only automobile, entirely designed and built in India. However, it was fashionable in those days to flaunt your foreign collaboration! Most were dependent on imported technology, CKD (Complete Knock Down) packs had to be just assembled and sold. Consumers considered a product made with foreign collaboration as 'tried and tested' and therefore would last for years and years, maybe for a generation! "Sturdiness" was the most important attribute of a vehicle. This meant that we had to bring out this attribute in the Luna as well.

Once again, we put on our thinking hats. We came up with some rather outrageous ideas too! We organized a rally of eight Luna riders to go "Around India in 80 days." My brother-in-law Kishore was one of the riders. They rode from Pune to Kashmir- Nepal-Assam- then all the way down south to Kanyakumari and were back in Pune on the appointed 80th day. Along the route, our dealers organized gala receptions and press conferences to publicize their progress. When they reached Pune, they rode a 'Victory Lap' in the city and were welcomed by Bollywood hero Sunil Dutt. This event went a long way in overcoming the doubts, if any, in people's minds about buying a product, which is totally indigenous, without any element of foreign collaboration.

Luna Invades America

After a stupendous success in the domestic market, we contemplated exporting Luna to America. The idea was that if Americans accept Luna, it would mean the product is world class and we would not have to worry about it not being made under foreign collaboration.

It finally happened through a mutual friend. We met an importer who was interested. In USA, everything is 'mega'! He placed an order for 1,000 vehicles!

At the time, we were unaware of a lot of laws and regulations regarding vehicles in the USA. The Luna had to be fitted with additional indicators all over! You needed tyre-wear indicator, brake- shoe indicator, better powered headlamps and more! To make matters worse, every state had a different law. We had to comply with state laws as well!

However, there was a big problem. The product liability laws of USA were extremely strict. In the event of an accident, the manufacturer was held entirely responsible and the penalty could run into millions of dollars.

I looked up the laws and found that the "importer" is also classified as the "manufacturer." I requested our importer to get an insurance cover for himself and that we would compensate him for this by reducing the cost of the Luna. Despite having to sell it at a lower price, we were happy about the volumes and the exposure that the Luna was gaining in the USA.

Americans have a do-it-yourself culture. So our approach to selling the Luna was very unique. We gave the buyer a kit which he himself could put together! This had two advantages: the packaging was simple and the containers could carry more vehicles!

We sold over 50,000 vehicles in the USA. They loved the Luna. One American guy rode on it from the East Coast to the West Coast! We established a strong setup for spares and support. We also went out of our way to assure 72-hour delivery of any part. Such commitment from our side ensured that we built trust among our buyers.

In one of the most audacious marketing moves at the time, we placed an advertisement for Luna in the *Time* magazine in the US. Those days, there was just the one World Edition of the magazine. It cost us two lakh rupees! The advertisement was headlined 'Luna Invades America'! When the issue hit newsstands in India, it was

a revelation to our buyers. It buried the 'no foreign collaboration' issue forever.

"Samay Bachaiye"

The value proposition of "Samay Bachaiye" jingle also
needed to be reinforced. We pitted the Luna against the
mighty Deccan Queen. A train that is synonymous with
speed and punctuality. A race was organised between
Deccan Queen and Luna. The Deccan Queen starts at
7.20 am from Pune Station and Luna would also start
at the same time. We requested Shri Jayantrao Tilak to
flag off the race and our challenge was to reach Dadar
station before the train. To give authenticity to the entire
activity, we invited the Police Commissioner of Mumbai
to be the judge. We won the race comfortably, thus dis-
pelling any doubts of its efficiency. The Luna actually
reached 20 minutes before the Deccan Queen!

The performance of the Luna in the race was outstand-
ing. Our car driver who was travelling behind the Luna
was unable to keep pace with it! To some, this may seem
gimmicky, but we were clear in the message we wanted
to send out. Our value propositions being "Samay
Bachaiye" (save time) and this activity underlined that
theme. If the Luna could beat the Deccan Queen, it was
indeed fast! Moreover, the race wasn't on a flat road but

through winding roads and ghats which made it a rather treacherous terrain in the days before the Expressway!

"Petrol Bachaiye"

To underline our next value proposition, we organized 'Stretch a Rupee' races. We put in petrol worth just Re 1 and challenged people to travel as far as they could. There were people who modified their vehicles! Some consumers made minimum friction vehicles; polished the tyres; cut down on the weight and so on. One person even sat on the chassis to reduce the drag!

Luna in Films and TV

I wanted to make a short film on Luna. I approached Mr Shyam Benegal, the internationally acclaimed film director. He quoted a sum which was much beyond our budget. When I grumbled a bit he suggested that we should consider taking new fresh faces instead of established actors and actresses. I agreed. When the short film was made, it had Shabana Azmi, Smita Patil and Mohan Agashe who were being introduced by Benegal in 'Ankur!' Since our short film was released before 'Ankur' I think we can claim that our short film on Luna was the debut film for Shabana Azmi and Smita Patil !

Sachin Tendulkar was an upcoming cricketer then. He was barely 15 years of age. We approached him to model for Luna. He readily agreed. I think that was the first ever endorsement he made.

In those days, product placements in films were not prevalent but we got some unexpected benefits when Luna was shown in a movie. Our dealer in Chennai had his showroom right opposite Gemini Studio and Tamil films showing stars riding the Luna got us some unexpected publicity. This led to another marketing brainwave! We encouraged our dealers in film cities to make the vehicles available at prominent movie studios, offering them for rides! We got a big fillip when Raj Kapoor called on us and asked for a pink coloured Luna for his movie 'Gopichand Jasoos.' Despite his bulky disposition, the Luna managed him just fine. In fact, a whole gang of hero and his friends in the movie were shown riding the Luna!

Subsequently, we sponsored the popular TV serial 'Surabhi.' The show used to be telecast all over India. We requested them to showcase the vehicle in every episode. To the viewer, the message that percolated was that the Luna is omnipresent! One day, they saw it in Khajuraho, another day in Kanyakumari! It was great!

Segmentwise Marketing

Through all our activities, we successfully communicated to the public that the Luna was a durable, economical and reliable vehicle. Despite this, we knew there were some segments we were not reaching out to, like shopkeepers, housewives and students. In those days, students often used bicycles to commute unlike today when two-wheelers are the norm. We were also keen to reach out to other middle-income groups like housewives and shopkeepers who were also mostly bicycle users.

One of our most innovative activity involved reaching out to shopkeepers. Our value proposition to this segment was fairly clear. In those days, assets below Rs 5,000 could be written off for income tax purpose. The Luna used to cost less than Rs 5,000. We suggested to a shopkeeper that he should buy a Luna for his assistant to do daily chores. Instead of perceiving Rs 5,000 as an added cost, we asked him to imagine that he was investing Rs. 5,000 and getting full tax benefit.

Once he was able to confirm this fact from his Tax Consultant, he was more than happy to buy! There were, of course, some who weren't convinced. We simply told them to look around and see how their competitors had already invested and benefited from this! That was the final convincing they needed!

Reaching to housewives posed its own unique challenge. So we decided to go where they congregated! Mahila Mandals (women's clubs) were our first halt! We went with women instructors and staff to give the women a demonstration of the Luna. In simple language, they would be explained the operation of the clutch and accelerator and so on. Armed with information and confidence that they could maintain this simple vehicle themselves, they could now ask their husbands to buy one for them! After all, riding it was as simple as riding a bicycle! We even went one step further and offered a refund of Rs 100 teaching fees or license fees if they bought the vehicle!

The value proposition for students was different. One summer, we sent letters to a batch of students who would be attending college from the next academic year. Our appeal to them was simple: buy a Luna and save time and energy! This was an instant connect with students who wanted to reach college on time and spend more time in the campus instead of having to run after buses or pedal all day long! To further incentivise them, we offered finance facilities. We covered all major colleges in Pune and sold over 100 in just one day - on the day colleges re-opened! Once the students reached college, we even set up Luna stands (like bicycle stands) so that the owners felt a sense of pride about their vehicles. The subliminal message propagated through this strategy, had a tremendous impact.

We also increased our presence through other activities. We created calendars, book covers and other such materials that were relevant to our audience. We were always present in college events and festivals and offered prizes to winners of student body elections and competitions as well. The prizes were as simple as T-shirts with LUNA emblazoned on them. The message that percolated was that if you are a winner, you will have a Luna. Of course, this had the rub-off effect of guys flaunting their victories to girls!

We also had special promotions around monsoons. We promoted the idea of making a short trip to Khandala on a Luna. If any girl student wanted to join the group but did not have a Luna, we offered it to her for the trip. This further created a buzz about Luna. Once they used it, they wanted to buy it for sure.

Direct Marketing

Direct marketing was yet to play a big role in those days. There was no TV and the Indian consumer still preferred to 'touch-and-feel' a product before they bought it. Having showrooms at every corner was not a viable solution. We felt that the time of direct marketing has arrived. We approached Dr. Anand Karandikar of Metrix Consultancy. He was a graduate of IIM-Ahmedabad. He liked our idea and formed a team to do Direct Marketing (DM). As a result, we sold literally hundreds of Lunas every month in every city where DM was implemented.

In order to make direct marketing work, we also had to arrange for finance. In those days, nationalized banks were not keen on offering individual loans! We developed an individual financing scheme with Citibank. We were the first to offer vehicle finance in the country and the first to take up the offer were small shopkeepers.

A story of firsts

As the market warmed up to Luna, creating top-of-mind awareness became important. This was achieved by us through many marketing firsts.

These marketing activities went a long way in establishing the Luna brand as trustworthy and a prized one. For instance, we were the first ever company in India to sponsor the 'Man of the Match Award' for test cricket matches. When the public saw their cricketing idols like B S Chandrasekhar, Farokh Engineer and Salim Durrani pose with Luna, it instantly drove an aspiration!

Similarly, we awarded a Luna to SSC (Class X) toppers. This associated us with 'being the best' and also endeared us to the student community – a large target for our products.

We were also the first two-wheeler manufacturers who set-up their network of Authorised Service Centres. This instilled a further sense of confidence about the company and its products.

Kinetic Honda

We faced a reverse situation in Kinetic Honda. The Kinetic Honda Scooter was made with foreign collaboration. However, it had to compete with long established scooters also made with foreign collaboration. How do we demonstrate to customers that our scooter was more reliable and dependable? We requested an independent organization to conduct an all-India 'run' with all the scooters in the market place and give the consumers an unbiased feedback about the breakdowns in the rally. To our delight, Kinetic Honda scooter came a topper. We publicized this fact widely to prove that our scooter was superior.

However, we felt we needed to do much more to create the Kinetic impact. We wanted to create world records with our scooter and here's how we did it! We entrenched ourselves in the Guinness Book of World Records. Mr and Mrs Shyla Yoganand crossed the Khardung La Pass in Ladakh, the highest motorable road in the world, on our scooter. That was the first time any scooter achieved such a feat. Thereafter, Mr Neville Darukhanawala, again a Pune resident, crossed 3000 km of Sahara desert on our scooter. We achieved another Guinness record. Finally Har Prakash Rishi and his team rode non-stop on Kinetic Honda scooter for 42 days at Sarasbaug, Pune. Officials of the Guinness Book of Records were invited to witness and assess the feat. We had another Guinness record in our kitty. We then sponsored a TV programme called "Guinness Book of World Records." That acted as a reminder to the viewers that our scooter was a world class one, a cut above the rest.

The scooter became so popular that we sold 1,000 of them in Pune City on a Dassera day.

We were very successful in exporting our scooters to Turkey and the Caribbean… the idea for this, in fact, came from our own Goa! In India, Goa is one place where two-wheelers are rented by foreign tourists to go to beaches from their hotels. Taking a cue from this, we decided to export the vehicle to similar markets overseas.

Market Learnings

It is important for every seller to penetrate the market, deep. It's not possible to stay away from the market and make plans. You need to be involved in executing the plans as well.

India is a 100 markets rolled into one. You need to make individual plans for every market. If you have a product which has one USP that you can communicate across the board, you are lucky! However, this is not true in most cases.

Study your market well. Know your market and respect your market's needs. There are a good number of reasons as to why a particular market behaves in a particular manner. You must study these.

Building your company

A s an entrepreneur, you need to have a vision that goes beyond horizons and an ear to the ground to ensure that your business is running smooth.

Starting off

There are many factors that will determine the success of your venture. It's important that you start off well. You should have Clear Plans for the present and a Vision for the future. Add Hard Work to that and you have a formula for success. However, Luck and Timing play an important part in the success your enterprise. So you should be always looking for opportunities and seize the moments that could have a game changing impact.

The Early Days

You, the entrepreneur are the driving force in the early days. You should use that period for getting hands-on experience of every facet of the working of your enterprise. That initial first-hand knowledge and hands-on experience will be your greatest strength. You may delegate the work later to your colleagues and may never have to do those activities ever again. Even then, the fact that you are fully knowledgeable about all aspects of the business will keep everyone on their toes and give you the results that you expect.

I remember when we had just started to export the Luna to the US, I accompanied one consignment. It was a proud moment for me, but on checking by the consignee, I was told that 10 vehicles were not starting! I hadn't taken a mechanic with us and hiring one locally would have been expensive and time-consuming since I would have had to tell him about the vehicle anyways. So the simplest solution was for me to solve the problem myself. It didn't matter that I was the Managing Director of the company. I knew everything about the product (the very first Luna was assembled by me) and I could troubleshoot it. This incident, in fact, instilled great faith about us in the buyer's mind.

As an entrepreneur, you need to be prepared for all eventualities. If you need to work overnight, you should.

Being a founder or MD or CEO shouldn't matter. The business always comes before everything else. Forget your social life for the early part of your business! Don't get ahead of yourself! You don't need a fancy office and a personal assistant on day one! Earn it.

Getting the right people

A trait that is essential in Mr. Right is that he should be result-oriented. For example, a salesman should sell. How he sells is not always important. He needs to have the ability to adjust, depending on the needs of the buyer. It doesn't have to be done in a textbook manner so long as the results are achieved. Everyone has his strengths and weaknesses. As long as the person is result oriented you can cover up for his weakness by giving him training or temporary help.

Great care has to be taken while hiring a person. At Kinetic Honda, our HR manager always visited applicant's home before hiring him to get a real sense of the person and why he wants to change jobs. We were also able to steer clear of problems by hiring persons from various communities and regions. This also ensured that there was no groupism of any kind.

Developing the people

We always believed that 50% of our managers should come from within the ranks. We groomed our shop floor workers to grow into managerial roles. They actually went up the ladder from workers to leading hands to chargemen to supervisors to foremen to managers. The advantage was that our managers had actual operating experience. We didn't have just desk managers.

It is important to rotate people within functions. People need time to show their abilities. Their existing circumstances may not be allowing them to deliver. We even moved Production staff into Sales department. Our Pithampur factory Chief Mr P.K. Sud was assigned the job of handling Sales in Maharashtra. Every industry and business will always have a period of downturn. We utilised these periods to rotate people and introduced them to know other skills. This actually showed a lot of people that they too possessed other skills that they weren't aware of themselves!

At Kinetic, I rotated the people regularly. I once temporarily put an Electronic Data Processing (EDP) manager in charge of engine assembly and he excelled at it! He was able to excel because he had an analytical mind and could understand the requirements and nuances of the new role.

Rotation is not welcomed by people, though! The way to handle it is to encourage them to understand the benefits of rotation. By knowing more and in detail about how other departments work, they could rise up to management positions. It is important to communicate this and make rotation a positive aspect of your HR practice.

Growing the company

We started Kinetic with a capital of just Rs 15 lakh. We did everything on our own. As a result, we were able to create a large knowledge base within the company. We created a culture of learning and one that accepted challenges. No task was impossible or unachievable. At Kinetic Honda, we started the other way around. Systems, processes and plans were in place from very early on. Everything worked like clockwork. Both models can work if done right. There isn't one way to do it.

Running a company is a cyclic process. In the early days, you have to grow the business. After the initial settling in period, the company will grow you as a professional. Once the company gets to a certain scale, you will start to learn how you have to grow. What worked for you in the past won't necessarily work going forward. This transformation also has to be visible in your outlook and demeanour - from a passionate-driven person to one who is in control of the situation. Once the company has grown to a certain level you can't be involved in all the processes on a daily basis. You have to aim to be an absentee boss. This means that the company should run without you. This will come about when you put strong systems and processes in place.

The Ecosystem

A major problem with a young workforce is attrition. Do announce that all your A Class employees will earn at least one Rupee more than the competition. Sure, this isn't a foolproof solution, but when most people are offered more than the competitor without having to look for a new job, it does solve the attrition problem to a large extent.

There are, of course, other issues due to which people will leave. Individual problems like distance to work-place are something you can't always tackle easily. For our factory in the PCMC area, most people in Pune had to travel for 30-40 minutes one way. Over a period of time, we actually started recruiting people from around our factory to get this problem out of the picture!

At Kinetic, we implemented many innovative policies. Our production facility is at Ahmednagar. We created a housing complex for our staff to make life comfortable for their families. We also do a few small things that makes their work enjoyable. We offer simple services like lunch dabba pickup from their home. A medical scheme is run where all medical expenses including hospitalisation are taken care of for the entire family of the workers. Children of the workers are given scholarships so that they continue their studies and do well in their lives.

At Kinetic Honda, we adopt the Japanese policy, like everyone wears the same uniform and all offices are open, that is, we have no cabins. Everyone eats in the same place and the same food is served. Everyone exercises early in the morning at the workplace. Workers are led by the section head and that shows leadership. It's not just about the exercise aspect. It's about spending time together as a team.

We extended our HR presence to show genuine care for our workers and anyone who called in sick. HR managers would personally visit homes of workers who called in sick. Yes, this served a dual purpose, but it also showed that the company cared! We continue this culture.

Some of the things that were imbibed into our culture through the Honda association were the importance of HR. There was a rule at Honda that senior management had to spend 30% of their time in HR! And the Japanese did enforce this rule too! They put a lot of emphasis on sharing feedback about performance with the staff. Whether good or bad, it was always shared in a timely manner to ensure that the output didn't suffer.

I remember a great story of how much importance the Japanese put on resource management. There was a visiting staffer from Japan whose father was unwell. The entire head office in Tokyo spent time and effort in planning his return trip to ensure he made it on time. That he refused to go without completing his work, is yet more proof of how such practices drive loyalty!

If you are a manufacturing or production company, you are also required to manage unions. At Kinetic Honda, we never treated them as a nuisance, rather as our partners. We developed a rapport with them that allowed us to work cordially. They showed us the utmost respect and always stood by us. We were able to create a bond with workers through facilities like doctors on campus, loans for scooters and so on. We were able to give them a little more than they would have got anywhere.

The Entrepreneur

The Entrepreneur should be clear about the kind of company he wants to create and the work culture he wants. The Entrepreneur sets the culture. And he needs to first set it by example.

The Entrepreneur should have a passion for what he is creating and doing.

The Entrepreneur ensures that his vision about the Company is shared on common ground.

He should be transparent about his company. He will share the good and the bad with the staff. If the company is going through a bad phase after a good period, it is important to share this. During the good times, everyone is happy! But the bad times is when character is tested. A company needs to tighten its belt when needed and people will understand it. Every person in the company who played his part in contributing to the success of the Company should be recognised during the good period. That recognition will help in tiding over the bad times.

The Entrepreneur should realize that people are important and they shouldn't be treated as machines. He should give clear and well-thought out directions. This is possible through clarity of thought. The ability to handle stress and do multiple things in a working day is important.

Even the Entrepreneur needs to keep learning. That attitude is essential. Stay open to the fact that learning comes from everywhere; not only from textbooks. Your goal should be to end everyday saying "I have learned something today" instead of thinking "I have achieved something today".

The Indian Entrepreneur should realize that there is wealth at the bottom of the pyramid. Understanding the needs of the Indian masses and providing affordable and lasting solutions to them is a glorious opportunity for the Entrepreneur. There are 1.2 billion Indians! That's a huge market to cater to.

Take the example of an autorickshaw driver in Pune who draws water from a lake and purifiers it, using Reverse Osmosis (RO) through the pressure generated by a compressor run by his autorickshaw engine when it is on the run. He delivers the water to his buyers at Re 1 per bottle! This is 15 times less than the price of bottled water! How does he manage that? His autorickshaw is used for collecting the water, filtering it and delivering the purified water. He has eliminated all the intermediaries. I think that is a great example of an Entrepreneur.

An Entrepreneur does things differently. He does things that make a difference in people's lives.

Innovation for the future

As the next generation of entrepreneurs searches for the next big idea, it's important to remember that there is a treasure at the bottom of the pyramid too! Everyone is looking to serve the technology enabled user and create products and services that will satiate the needs of the few. But those who have little is a majority. And by finding a solution to their most common problems, there is a greater impact to be made – socially and financially.

Energy is an aspect of our lives that is becoming critical. Generating or creating more energy is going to be harder by the day. What we do have in abundance that we can leverage is solar energy. Despite this, we face a power deficit. There is a definite demand for someone to invent a way to capture, channelize and distribute solar energy in an efficient manner for everyday use.

Photovoltaic devices are becoming increasingly cheaper and it is time to put these to good use and create individual energy storage and distribution mechanism. Currently, we lose over 30% of the energy generated due to the distribution methods in use. Imagine every rooftop having the ability to capture solar energy and create electricity. This can be distributed within the household as DC (as opposed to the current AC that is converted to DC by various devices causing wastage). This will ensure that wastage is minimized since we are creating our own power and the dependence on buying it will also be greatly reduced thereby easing the pressure on our limited natural resources.

To make this a reality, we should fight for having a DC home with fans, lights and other electrical appliances running on DC power supply. Almost all home appliances like computer, TV, air conditioners, refrigerators can run on DC and solar energy can be used to power these appliances. This helps us save and use energy more efficiently.

Other than the need of power, we must focus on the issue of waste management. India has one of the world's largest populations. Therefore, the daily waste generated is immense. With the rise in population, the density of population has also increased creating huge volumes of waste in relatively small areas – mostly urban.

It is possible to use this waste and generate energy – electricity – as well. At this stage, it does require more research, but it's not impossible. By continually working towards energy efficient appliances and easier means of creating energy, it will benefit various sectors including healthcare especially in rural areas where power availability and quality are both poor. Not only will this bring down the cost of the appliances ensuring availability across India, but also create an assured way for the devices and appliances to be used where they are required and make quality healthcare available at affordable prices.

Transport is another area in India that requires serious attention. We have among the world's largest river networks, but also, the poorest used! Presently, we depend upon rail transport and ground transport, thereby driving the demand for natural energy. River navigation has to be seriously planned and worked on as it costs about a third of the other modes. The various interconnecting rivers will ensure high connectivity for transport of goods and people.

While this may present the argument that our rivers carry drinking water, we must reduce our dependence on them and revert to the ancient method of creating wells. For long, India relied on wells for drinking water and other household needs. Now, the country is investing in building dams to store excess water. In dams and lakes, there is a huge loss of water due to evaporation. Moreover, wells offer additional advantages of natural filtration and endless storage!

Seeing how our economy is still largely an agrarian one, it is important to ensure rainfall is timely and adequate. Science has given us the option to ensure this happens through artificial rain-making, aka cloud seeding.

All this requires is the introduction of silver iodide into ready clouds and delayed or deficient monsoons may be a thing of the past. Western economies haven't given enough importance to researching this since they have abundant rains and water. As a result, we have also ignored it, whereas it could have been the solution to our rain problems. There is still time to set this right.

Yet another focus area for India should be genetically modified foods. This has, unfortunately, become a bad word. For ages, now, we have been exposed to genetically modified food. The trouble is when food is modified to suit needs of large companies who want to sell their fertilisers or seeds or other products. If modification will ease the burden on the farmer and allow him to create the same crop using less water, then it's a good development.

If Indian scientists can research on the subject and thoroughly test the crop varieties before making them commercially available, it will prove to be a big boon to not just farmers, but also to the consumer at large.

Similar to some of the ideas presented above, there is much possible across various sectors. Find a problem and try to solve it. Be innovative, be relentless.

Inspirations

My father was my biggest inspiration. He was a born entrepreneur. Even during his final days, he was keen about how things worked! Even when in hospital, he was more interested in showing me how a particular bed mechanism worked. He actually made me draw the mechanism in four different positions! He was a born creator.

There are a lot of our colleagues who have inspired me and taught me a lot. I am an Electrical Engineer by education. We had Mr Daljit Singh Bomrah who worked with us. We had recruited him for our welding tools machine. During my conversations with him, I realised that he had a lot of knowledge and common sense. We went around seeing how to design some mechanism.

Together, we learned how to create specification sheets for new products. That he wasn't even a graduate made me realise that he isn't a born mechanical engineer and neither am I. But if he can learn and make things happen, so can I!

We had hired a gentleman from TVS, Mr Vepa Murari. He was a genius at all things electrical! How to use the knowledge you have gained from books is an art. He would bring down every problem to a formula and solve it! So without depending on anyone else, he would take his time and solve any problem we gave him.

Another colleague who inspired me was Mr S N Kulkarni. I remember throwing a problem at him one day. I told him, "Digital TV and computer both have audio and video circuits. So why can't we have same circuit work for computer and TV?" His response was not to agree or disagree but to ask for time to study the theory. One week later, he came back and confirmed that it was possible. He said he could design a circuit that could function as a TV and computer! The result of this was the Merlin TV.

It is easy to agree or disagree with any theory, but to confirm after getting thorough information and studying a problem is what is inspiring. This made me realise that the people around us are intelligent and willing to go the extra mile. That is inspiring.

Never-ending Innovation

Not all innovations see the light of day. Through my life, I have worked on a variety of projects, each with the aim of improving everyday life for the public.

At Kinetic itself, we had worked on a wide range of innovations for our vehicles. We had created a Kinetic Honda with a canopy to protect the rider from rain and sun! We had also worked on a concept for seat coolers that would make the first 10 minutes of the ride comfortable for anyone during the hot Indian summers! The marketability for these, however, was not always guaranteed. As a result, we didn't commercially produce many such innovations.

As a matter of fact, innovation beyond our products is something we have always been keen on driving. Some of the more interesting concepts we have worked on, includes a bed cooler that will allow the comfort of an air conditioner to the common man. A concept like this needs great detail in planning. The idea was simple: You need an underground water tank which most houses have. When this water is transported through a pipe to an overhead tank, it can be routed through the bedroom and a pipe can carry it around your bed making it cool! This is the sort of 'natural' innovation that can solve a lot of people's problems.

Innovation is a long, arduous path. You need to have motivation and vision to change habits that will lead to your innovation becoming the norm. History has proof of this being a successful tactic. The British used this very successfully and got Indians hooked to tea! Until then, tea produced in India was mainly exported to Britain. But they realised that there is a huge market right here in India. Indians weren't fond of tea but the British started giving it free once a week to get us Indians to like the taste. And soon enough, it became a habit!

As an entrepreneur, you can do different things or do things differently. Remember, that it has to make a difference in people's lives. That will be a sure way to ensure success. Our products have always been path breaking and ones that helped people improve their quality of life.

In conclusion, I would like to end with a quote, "just as energy is the basis of life itself, and ideas the source of innovation, so is innovation the vital spark of all human change, improvement and progress."

Notes

Notes